Animal World

Deer

Pl

D1243035

Donna Bailey and Christine Butterworth

STECK-VAUGHN
LIBRARY
A Division of Steck-Vaughn Company

All summer, this stag has lived
in a herd with other stags.
Now it is fall in the forest.
It is time for the stag to find
a female deer, a doe.

2

In the fall when it is time to mate,
stags often travel a long way
to find does.
They jump over fences and cross rivers.

Here, stags have found a herd of does
and young deer.

The stag chooses a doe as his mate.
He rubs his antlers against a tree.
Then he is ready to mate with her.

By the next spring, the doe is ready
to have her baby.
She leaves the herd to find a quiet place
for her baby to be born.

A baby deer is called a fawn.
This fawn has just been born.
The fawn's mother licks it clean.

The fawn lies by its mother.
It is only ten minutes old, but
it already knows how
to drink its mother's milk.

After about half an hour, the doe
pushes the fawn with her nose
to help it stand up.
The fawn's legs are wobbly at first.

Here the fawn is four days old.

It can run and walk much better now.

The doe and fawn join the herd again.

The white spots on the fawn's coat
help hide the fawn from its enemies.
The fawn will lose these spots when
it is six weeks old.

For eight months, the fawn stays
with its mother and drinks her milk.
Then it learns to eat leaves and grass.
The doe shows it which plants
are safe to eat.

12

An older doe is the leader of the herd.
She stamps her foot to warn the herd
of danger.
Then the does and fawns run and hide.

In the summer, the deer have
lots of food to eat.
They swallow their food
and store it in their stomachs.

14

When the deer are resting, they bring food
up from their stomachs and
chew it again, the way cows do.
This is called chewing the cud.
Deer use four stomachs to eat like this!

When the fawns are about one year old,
some of them begin to grow antlers.
These are the young stags.
Only stags grow antlers.

The young stags stay with their mothers
until they are two years old.
Then the does send the young stags to live
with the herd of older stags.

Stags use their antlers for
defense and to fight other stags
during the mating season.
The mating time of year is called the rut.

18

When two stags want to mate with
the same doe, they fight each other.
They lock their antlers together and
push hard to see which stag is stronger.
The weaker stag runs away.

Before spring comes, the stags
lose their antlers.
The antlers fall off so that the stags
can grow new, longer antlers.

20

Soon after the stag loses its old antlers,
small bumps appear on the stag's head.
These bumps are the new antlers growing.
The bone in the new antlers is still soft.

The new antlers are covered with
a soft furry skin called velvet.
The velvet protects the antlers
as they grow.

The new antlers have more branches and points than the old antlers.

By early summer, the stag's new antlers
are fully grown.
The bone is now hard.
The velvet dries up and peels off.

Deer live in different parts of the world.
This is the world's smallest deer, the pudu,
which lives in the Andes.
It is only one foot tall.

The largest deer is the moose.

Its huge antlers are about six feet across.

The male or bull moose can be as tall as seven feet and can weigh up to 2,000 pounds.

Moose live in Alaska and Canada.
In the summer, they eat the twigs and
leaves from trees.
They also wade into lakes
to eat water plants.

In the winter, the moose keep a patch of
ground clear of snow.
This is called a moose yard.
The moose scrape away the snow with
their antlers and hooves to find
moss and lichen to eat.

Lapland in northern Europe also
has lots of snow in the winter.
The Lapp people raise reindeer
for their meat and for
their rich milk.

The Inuit people of Canada and Alaska
call their reindeer caribou.
Caribou have thick hair to keep them warm.
They even have hairy noses!

Caribou travel long distances across Alaska. They walk from their summer feeding grounds in the Arctic to their winter feeding grounds in the Canadian forests.

In most kinds of deer,
only the males grow antlers.
In herds of caribou and reindeer,
both stags and does grow antlers.

Index

Reading Consultant: Diana Bentley
Editorial Consultant: Donna Bailey
Executive Editor: Elizabeth Strauss
Project Editor: Becky Ward

Picture research by Jennifer Garratt
Designed by Richard Garratt Design

Photographs
Cover: OSF Picture Library (Leonard Lee Rue III)
Bruce Coleman: 2,4,5,7,8,9,10,11,12,16,17,19,24,27 (Leonard Lee Rue III), 3,6,15,21,22 (Erwin & Peggy Bauer), 13,23 (R. Carr), 14 (Stephen Krasemann), 20 (Hans Reinhard), 25 (Francisco Erize), 28 (James Simon), 29 (B&C Alexander), 30 (Stephen Kaufman), 31 (Nicholas Devore)
OSF Picture Library: title page (Leonard Lee Rue III), 18,26,32 (Stan Osolinski)

Library of Congress Cataloging-in-Publication Data: Butterworth, Christine. Deer / Christine Butterworth and Donna Bailey. p. cm.—(Animal world) Includes index. SUMMARY: Presents the life cycle of a deer and also depicts relatives pudu, moose, reindeer, and caribou. ISBN 0-8114-2638-6 1. Deer—Juvenile literature. [1. Deer.] I. Bailey, Donna. II. Title. III. Series. QL737.U55B82 1990 599.73'57—dc20 90-9960 CIP AC

ISBN 0-8114-2638-6
Copyright 1991 Steck-Vaughn Company
Original copyright Heinemann Children's Reference 1991

2 3 4 5 6 7 8 9 0 LB 96 95 94 93 92 91